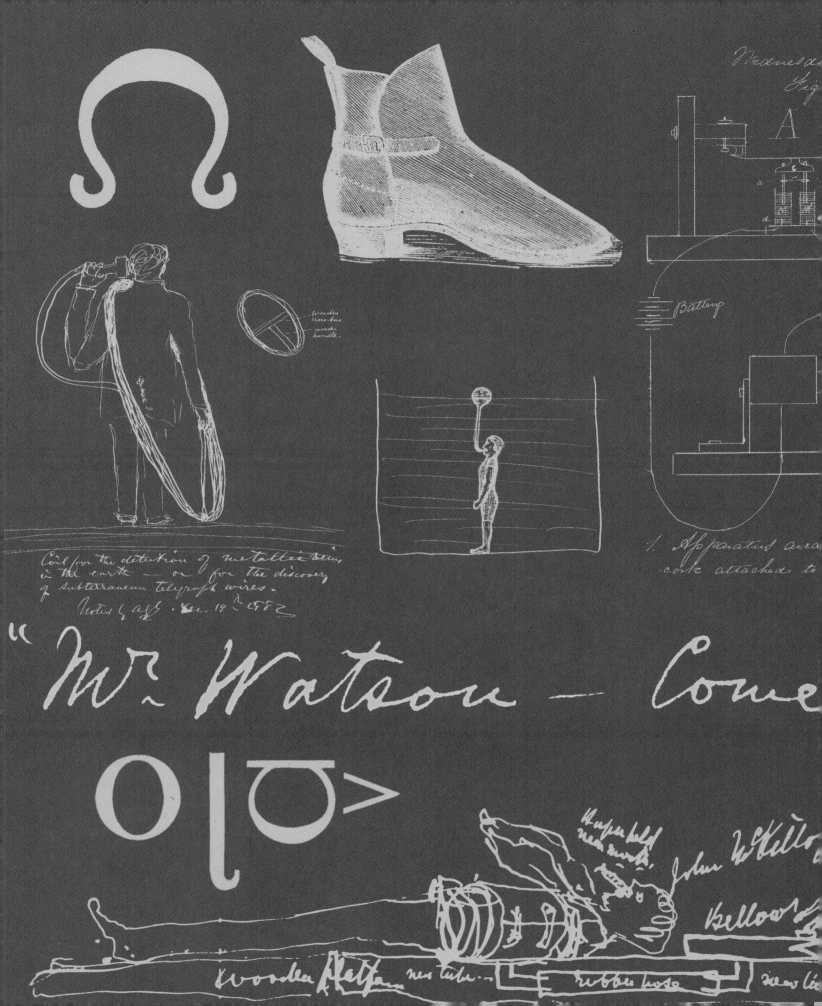

Coil for the detection of metallic veins in the earth — or for the discovery of subterranean telegraph wires.

"M̄r Watson — Come

A finger-spelling glove made by
Alexander Graham Bell.
See page 15

The ear phonautograph led to
the invention of the telephone.
See page 20

This is a replica of the first
working telephone.
See page 26

This plane set a world record
for long-distance flying.
See pages 52–53

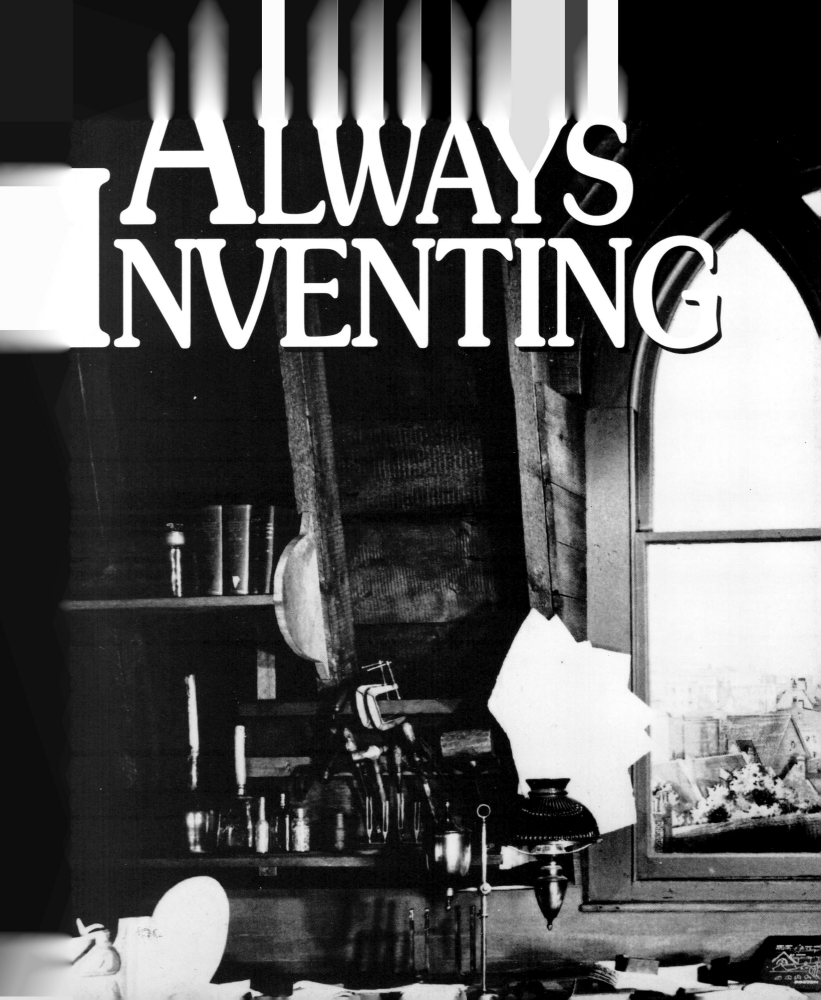

A PHOTOBIOGRAPHY OF ALEXANDER GRAHAM BELL

BY TOM L. MATTHEWS

NATIONAL GEOGRAPHIC SOCIETY
Washington, D.C.

For all my friends from Chesterbrook

Front jacket: Always inventing, Alexander Graham Bell makes laboratory notes
in his study. The inset picture shows him in 1892 making the first
New York to Chicago call on a commercial line.

Back jacket: Bell with his grandson Melville Bell Grosvenor, who grew to love science
and learning through his grandfather's example

Title page: A reconstruction of the Boston laboratory where Bell invented the telephone

Page 6: An energetic Bell plays with his granddaughters Gertrude *(left)*,
Lilian, and Mabel Grosvenor.

Published by the National Geographic Society
1145 17th Street N.W.
Washington, D.C. 20036

John M. Fahey, Jr.
*President and
Chief Executive Officer*

Gilbert M. Grosvenor
Chairman of the Board

Nina D. Hoffman
Senior Vice President

William R. Gray
*Vice President and Director
of the Book Division*

Staff for this book:

Suzanne Patrick Fonda
Editor

Jennifer Emmett
Assistant Editor

Marianne Koszorus
Art Director

David M. Seager
Designer

Carl Mehler
Director of Maps

Michelle H. Picard
Map Production

Kristin M. Edmonds
Researcher

Anne Marie Houppert
Indexer

Vincent P. Ryan
Manufacturing Manager

Richard S. Wain
Production Manager

Library of Congress Cataloging-in-Publication Data
Matthews, Tom, 1949–
        Always inventing : a photobiography of Alexander Graham Bell / by Tom L. Matthews
                p. cm.
Includes bibliographical references and index.
        Summary: A biography, with photographs and quotes from Bell himself, which follows
this well known inventor from his childhood in Scotland through his life long efforts to come up with ideas
that would improve people's lives.
        ISBN 0-7922-7391-5
        1. Bell, Alexander Graham, 1847–1922—Juvenile literature. 2. Bell, Alexander Graham,
1847–1922—Portraits—Juvenile literature. 3. Inventors—United States—Biography—Juvenile literature.
[1. Bell, Alexander Graham, 1847–1922. 2. Inventors.]
I. Title.
TK6143.B4M37   1999
621.385'092—dc21   98-27209

Printed in the United States of America

"Wherever you may find the inventor, you may give him wealth or you may take from him all that he has; and he will go on inventing. He can no more help inventing than he can help thinking or breathing."

FOREWORD

IMAGINE THE EXCITEMENT, PRIDE, and incentive to invent that Alexander Graham Bell felt when, at age 11, he found a way to help a millowner separate the husk from a kernel of wheat. Little did he know that it would be the start of a long journey to fame. My great-grandfather thoroughly enjoyed unraveling the secrets of science and spent his life striving to find ways to improve the quality of life for people everywhere. Of course, the telephone is his best known invention. Fortunately for him, proceeds from it allowed him to live his life exactly as he pleased: teaching the deaf, inventing, and enjoying his family, especially his grandchildren.

My father, Melville Bell Grosvenor, was his first grandchild. Bell devoted a full page in one of his many notebooks to a birth announcement. It was sandwiched between notes for a speech on heredity and studies for tetrahedral kites! As a boy, my father spent most of his summers at Beinn Bhreagh, or "Beautiful Mountain," Bell's home on Nova Scotia's Cape Breton Island. Bell enjoyed spending time there with all of his grandchildren and was always encouraging them to experiment. He considered childhood "the great observing period in human life," and the child as "an explorer in a new land in which marvelous discoveries may be made each day."

Bell's enthusiasm for learning and experimenting was shared by his beloved wife, Mabel. She shielded her husband from the mundane crises in life and encouraged his work with helicopters, hydrofoils, jet airplanes, and even rocket ships. Their marriage, their partnership, and their love were brilliant right to the end.

Fortunately for all of us, my great-grandfather recorded everything, sketched every idea, documented every experiment. His *Lab Notes,* the *Beinn Bhreagh Recorder*, and other volumes total almost 150,000 documents, which reside at the Library of Congress, in Washington, D.C. Hundreds of his inventions, models, and kites are beautifully displayed in the Alexander Graham Bell Museum in Baddeck, Nova Scotia. Parks Canada has created the best, most complete collection of any 20th-century inventor, all set on the shores of Bell's beloved Bras d'Or Lakes. I urge you to visit these places and experience for yourself the magic of the man whose "talking machine" changed the world.

Gilbert M. Grosvenor

Gilbert M. Grosvenor
Chairman, National Geographic Society

LUCKILY FOR US, nobody in Alexander Graham Bell's family ever seemed content with things as they were.

Grandfather Bell was born into a family of Scottish shoemakers in 1790. Dissatisfied with the shoe trade, he took up acting and studied literature, grammar, and speech. He became a superb elocutionist, or public speaker, and eventually taught speech. He must have been an extremely good teacher to get aristocrats in London to pay a common, self-educated Scotsman for English lessons.

His son, Alexander Melville (Melville), made a career in speech, too. He fell in love with and married Eliza Grace Symonds. They had three children and divided their time between a large city apartment in Edinburgh, Scotland, and Milton Cottage in the nearby countryside.

Their middle child, Alexander (Alec), was born into a vibrant, energy-filled environment on March 3, 1847. Edinburgh buzzed with scientific theory and invention. Alec's father was a leading intellectual who lectured and taught but wanted to do even more.

A young Alexander Bell poses with his father, Alexander Melville Bell, and his grandfather, Alexander Bell. He gave himself the middle name Graham at age 11 in tribute to a friend.
Left: A confident 17-year-old Alec.

Eliza Symonds Bell painted this fanciful miniature of her three sons: Melville, Edward, and Alexander. *Right:* The family poses outside Milton Cottage. Alec called it "my real home in childhood."

Melville Bell doggedly pursued a goal that had frustrated speech professionals for more than a century: creating a universal phonetic alphabet, an alphabet of symbols that represented any sound the human voice could make. It took years of trial and error, but Melville Bell finally perfected his Visible Speech system in 1864.

Alec's mother was a painter of miniature portraits who loved playing the piano even though she was very nearly deaf. By putting her ear tube on the soundboard of the piano, she could hear, or feel, the music. Alec showed natural talent for music, and his mother encouraged him to develop it.

At age 11 Alec devised his first invention. Challenged by his best friend's father, a millowner, to "do something useful," he made a tool to clean the tough husks from wheat kernels. His "taking off husks" didn't set the world on its ear, but it gave him confidence in his ability to understand and solve technological problems.

Alec loved exploring nature—collecting plants and dissecting dead animals. Although known by his friends as the Professor of Anatomy, he struggled at school with Latin, Greek, and the like.

His father thought a change of scene might help, so at age 15, Alec went to spend a year studying with his grandfather.

He called the experience "the turning point of my whole career." Grandfather Bell demanded mature, adult behavior and got it. Alec soon dressed, acted, and thought like a much older person. And like a Bell, he excelled in elocution and enjoyed public speaking.

Alec returned to Edinburgh hungry for both achievement and independence. He thought of running away to sea, but instead applied for a position teaching music and elocution at a boarding school in Elgin. His father gave him a recommendation, and in 1863 Alec was off to the northern coast of Scotland.

During the next four years he had several teaching jobs, took university classes, and helped his father demonstrate his Visible Speech system.

The first of two family tragedies that would shape Alec's future happened in 1867 when his younger brother Edward died from tuberculosis, a bacterial infection of the lungs. After that, Alec spent more time at home and began using Visible Speech to teach deaf students.

In 1870 Melly, Alec's older brother, also died from tuberculosis. There was no cure for the disease then, and it flourished in the cold, wet climate of England and Scotland. Doctors considered Alec at risk.

Melville Bell had a plan to save his last living son: The family would move to Canada. As a teenager, Melville had been sent there for his health. He found the weather excellent and the "go-ahead" North American way of life invigorating. Melville and Eliza begged Alec to join them. Reluctantly, he did.

The Bells sailed to Canada and bought a home in southern Ontario, near Brantford, in August 1870.

Alec's parents gave him a love of photography and music. Alec made this picture of Melly *(above, left)* and a friend in disguises. He may have played the horn *(right),* but piano was his true love. He learned new pieces well into his 70s.

These Visible Speech symbols spell out words. Each symbol represents a sound the human mouth can produce. By learning to speak these symbols, a person with no English could say "shoe," "hat," or any other word. Alec used the system to teach the deaf to speak. *Opposite:* Alec made this finger-spelling glove for George Sanders. By pointing to the letters on the glove, Alec could communicate with George in public without it being obvious that the boy was deaf.

"I find myself making headway every day....I look to the establishment of a good profession here—"

ALEC FELT REFRESHED, recovered, and restless within a few months. His father's recommendation helped him land a job teaching at the Boston School for Deaf Mutes. His success with teaching Visible Speech led to a position as a professor of vocal physiology at Boston University. In addition to his classes, he tutored students in the evenings.

Alec remained close to two of his pupils all his life. George Sanders was born deaf. At age five he had no speech and couldn't communicate with anyone. Alec made a glove with the alphabet written on it to teach George spelling.

George Sanders

Mabel Hubbard was the daughter of Gertrude and Gardiner Greene Hubbard. Scarlet fever had made Mabel totally deaf at age five. She knew how to speak and her parents were anxious for her to continue to speak as normally as possible. They did not want her to learn sign language, the recommended means of communication for the deaf at the time. After a decade of searching for the right teacher, the Hubbards found Alec Bell. Intelligent, well-educated, and eager, Mabel made astounding progress.

Mabel Hubbard

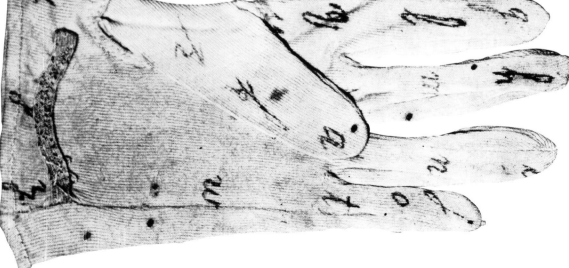

"I used to tell my friends that some day we should speak by telegraph."

Understanding the science that made human speech possible had fascinated Alec from a very early age. As teenagers, Alec and his brother Melly had actually used the larynx, or voice box, of a dead sheep to create a speaking machine. Modeled on the human mouth and throat, it cried "Mama" convincingly enough to attract the attention of their neighbors.

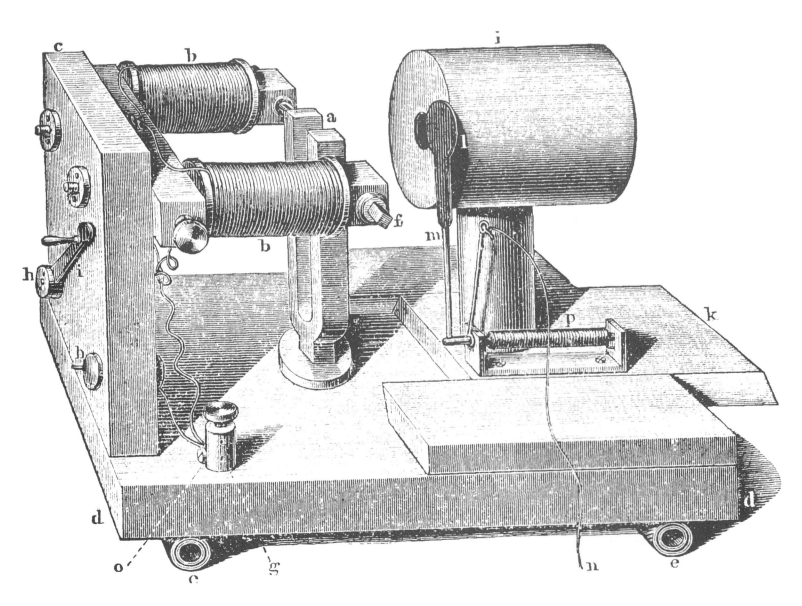

While teaching at Elgin, Alec had investigated the pitch, or vibrating speed, of vowel sounds using musical tuning forks. He discovered that each vowel had a unique rate of vibration. Alec was disappointed to find that his experiments just duplicated those of the famous German scientist Hermann von Helmholtz. Helmholtz's work was published only in German, which Alec couldn't read, but from diagrams in the book he determined that Helmholtz had used electricity to transmit, or send, vowel sounds through a wire.

Alec was inspired. If vowels could travel through wire, then consonants could. If the parts of words could be transmitted, why not words and sentences?

It was all a mistake, but a very fortunate one. Alec had misunderstood the diagrams in Hemholtz's book, but his belief in the idea that sound had been transmitted electrically guided him down paths of experimentation that led to the invention of the telephone.

The telegraph had produced a mid-century revolution in communications: Messages traveled by wire rather than by horseback or train or ship. But by 1872 the telegraph's limitations were clear.

Alec *(above)* mistakenly believed that a device *(left)* made by Hermann von Helmholtz not only produced vowel sounds but also transmitted them. Alec's experiments with sound led him from Helmholtz to this harmonic telegraph receiver *(right)*, which showed him that an electric current could carry sound through wire.

Only one message at a time could be carried on a line between cities. Messages lined up to get onto the wire, and the cost of sending telegrams was too high for personal use. Telegraphy was primarily a business tool.

It was obvious to Alec and already established inventors like Thomas Edison and Elisha Gray that multiple messaging was the technology to aim for. The inventor of a multiple telegraph would improve communication for everybody and get rich for his efforts.

There was no better place than Boston for Alec's experiments. The city tingled with ideas, inventors, and enthusiasm. It hummed with workshops making electrical devices.

Alec competed with the inventors Thomas Edison (seated below, center, with hat and kerchief) and Elisha Gray (right, in front row, with an invention on his lap) and their large workshops.

Alec taught during the day and invented at night. He was making progress on a multiple telegraph that he called a harmonic telegraph. His concept was that many messages could be sent simultaneously through a single wire if they were all sent at different pitches and decoded by receivers each tuned to a specific pitch. He devoured books from the library. The Massachusetts Institute of Technology loaned him a laboratory to work in, and he tested his ideas on some of the scientists he knew.

At his parents' Brantford home in the summer of 1874, he tried improving the phonautograph, a machine that drew the shapes of sounds by tracing their vibrations with a pen. Alec thought the machine would help him teach the deaf to speak. Instead, it helped him discover the principle of the telephone.

"*I have scarce dared to breathe [the idea] to anybody for fear of being thought insane. I was uncertain of the fundamental principle.*"

The phonautograph showed Alec that sound was made up of a series of waves. He reasoned that if sound waves could make a pen draw patterns on glass, they might be able to generate an electric current—an "undulatory" electric current that would rise and fall according to the pitch, or speed of vibration, of a sound. He wrote, "If I could make a current of electricity vary in intensity precisely as the air varies in density during the production of sound, I should be able to transmit speech telegraphically."

An "on" or "off" current was used in telegraphy to send coded messages—dots and dashes that represented letters of the alphabet. Alec was suggesting that the complex rising and falling human voice could be converted into a continuous rising and falling, or undulatory, electric current and then be converted from electrical energy back into sound at the end of the wire. Alec had described the fundamental principle of the telephone. He hadn't discovered any new scientific ideas, but he had put existing ideas together in a way no one had before.

He had a theory but would it really work? He didn't know if undulatory current would carry sound over long distances. He didn't have the expertise at that moment to make a machine that would prove his theory, but he would try. He was an inventor. He had been one since age 11 when he made a machine that husked wheat.

In 1874 Alec experimented with the ear phonautograph. He attached a stalk of hay to a bone in a human ear and spoke into the ear. The sound made the hay trace a wavy line on the glass below. Alec thought that sound waves could be converted into an undulatory electric current and carried through a wire.

"*I feel as if I may yet* TAKE OFF SOME HUSKS!!!"

Alec needed resources: supplies, money, a technician to build things. Thomas Sanders and Gardiner Greene Hubbard, the fathers of Bell's speech pupils, saw that serious, hard-driving Alec had a worthwhile idea. They were eager to be his partners, gladly paying for supplies and an assistant. They would not pay Alec a salary, though. Sanders and Hubbard knew that their lone inventor was in a race with with the likes of Edison and Gray, and they wanted him to need to win.

In January 1875 Thomas Watson became Alec's assistant. He was a skilled craftsman and electrician, able to turn Alec's sketches into machines quickly. He grew to admire Bell and wrote, "no finer influence than Graham Bell ever came into my life."

Thomas Sanders   Gardiner Greene Hubbard

Spurred by ambition and Hubbard's warnings that he was competing with other inventors, Alec and Watson worked feverishly to produce a multiple telegraph. But Elisha Gray beat them to it and received the patent instead. In Washington for the patent application process, Alec arranged an interview with Joseph Henry, a respected electrical scientist. Alec told Professor Henry about his ideas for the transmission of speech using undulatory current. The professor called it "the germ of a great invention." When Alec said he lacked the understanding of electricity necessary to work out the practical problems, Henry urged him to "get it!"

Back in Boston, Alec and Watson tried dozens of combinations of electric current and materials to transmit it. They had no directions or blueprints to follow, so progress was painfully slow. Alec filled notebooks with the records of failed experiments but felt they were getting closer.

Undaunted, Alec wrote, "I think the transmission of the human voice is much more nearly at hand than I had supposed."

Sanders and Hubbard, the fathers of Alec's pupils, saw the potential of his ideas and eagerly became his partners. They hired Thomas Watson as his assistant.

Thomas Watson

"I have accidentally made a discovery of the very greatest importance...."

ON JUNE 2, 1875 ALEC AND WATSON were "tuning" the reeds in multiple telegraph transmitters and receivers. The reeds were thin, metal strips made to produce a single, pure tone when plucked. Suddenly, an accident happened that was actually a breakthrough.

With the electric current turned off, Watson plucked the reed on a receiver while, in the next room, Alec heard very faint noises coming from the transmitter that was connected to Watson's receiver. He was very surprised. The sound he heard was the pitch of Watson's reed. Alec also heard overtones, not a single, pure tone.

Alec knew instantly that a single reed, when vibrated, could induce enough undulatory current to send sounds as complex as the human voice from one room to another. Because of his perfect musical pitch and sensitive hearing, Alec heard what most people simply wouldn't have heard. Complex sounds, like the human voice, could induce a current, travel through a wire, and become sounds again at the other end of the wire. At that moment, Alexander Graham Bell became the first person to understand how and why a telephone would work.

He quickly sketched a machine that, because of its shape, he called the gallows telephone and had Watson build a pair. Although it couldn't carry conversations, the device did transmit complex sounds.

This scene of Alec and Watson in their workshop was painted by W. A. Rogers for a public that couldn't get enough inside information about the telephone and its inventor. The owl is a "portrait" of Alec painted by his fiancée, Mabel Hubbard. Alec's habit of working through the night reminded her of the owl's nocturnal behavior.

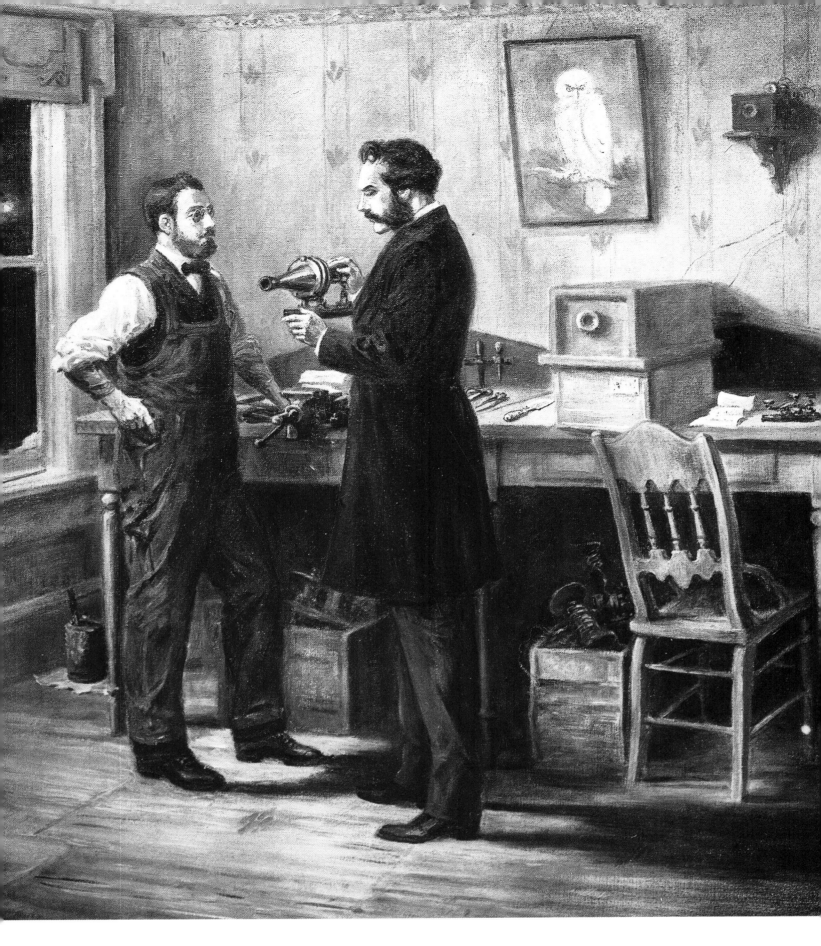

Hubbard, fearing that Elisha Gray or another inventor would file for a patent before they did, insisted that Alec prepare an application as quickly as possible. Alec worked on it for months until the impatient Hubbard finally filed the unfinished application on February 14, 1876.

Elisha Gray filed for a "speaking telegraph" less than two hours later the same day. Alec's patent application was better because it called for producing an undulatory current that would transmit the

THIS MODEL OF BELL'S FIRST TELEPHONE IS A DUPLICATE OF THE INSTRUMENT THROUGH WHICH SPEECH SOUNDS WERE FIRST TRANSMITTED ELECTRICALLY, 1875.

human voice. Gray's specifications used similar ideas, but they did not add up to a functional telephone.

Alec's device would work. Gray's would not.

Alexander Graham Bell received a patent called "Improvements in Telegraphy" on March 7, 1876. Bell, Hubbard, Sanders, and Watson would share in the money made from it. Those four had the exclusive right to make and sell telephones in the United States for 19 years.

Of course, Alec and Watson still had to make a telephone that could carry a conversation; a telephone that people would pay to use. That happened three days later, on March 10, 1876.

Using yet another new design, Alec made communications history when he said: "Mr. Watson—Come here—I want to see you."

In his lab notebook, Alec wrote that "to my delight he came and declared that he had heard and understood what I had said."

Left: This is a replica of the gallows telephone, the device Alec sketched on June 2, 1875. At right is a replica of the telephone that carried Alec's message to Watson. Alec spoke into the large opening. Watson heard him through a duplicate device in another room.

"I have discovered that my interest in my dear pupil...has ripened into a far deeper feeling...."

IN JUNE 1875, THE SAME MONTH ALEC heard Watson pluck the reed, he discovered that Mabel Hubbard was going away for the summer. The idea of separation made Alec recognize his love for Mabel. He immediately told her parents and his. Both families objected.

Alec's parents feared that the couple would have deaf children and were relieved to find out that Mabel hadn't been born deaf. The Hubbards thought Alec was much too old for their daughter. They were surprised to learn that he was only 28 years old. Alec was so intense and serious, they'd thought he was at least ten years older than that. More important, they didn't believe Alec could support their daughter properly as a teacher. Only the commercial success of Alec's inventions could make him acceptable as a son-in-law.

And Mabel? Was she overwhelmed with joy to hear about Alec's feelings?

No! She was unsure whether she could ever feel love for Alec, even though she regarded him very highly as a teacher. She wrote to him that "perhaps it is best we should not meet awhile now, and that when we do meet we should not speak of love."

Refusing to be discouraged, Alec visited Mabel and wrote to her constantly. More than a year later she accepted his proposal on Thanksgiving Day, 1876—her 18th birthday.

Alec promoted the telephone through paid lectures in 1877. This newspaper illustration shows Alec in Salem, Massachusetts, speaking to Tom Watson in Boston. Alec made $149 from this lecture, the first money he earned from the telephone. The next day he spent $85 to have a miniature silver telephone made for Mabel.

29

THIS TICKET
ONLY
GOOD FOR ONE
DAILY ADMISSION
THE HOLDER
WILL
OBTAIN A PASS CHECK
ON LEAVING
THE GROUNDS TO
RETURN.

NOT TRANSFERABLE

The first public demonstration of the telephone was at the Centennial Exhibition in Philadelphia on June 25, 1876. The scientific judges were stunned by Alec's achievement and voted him a certificate of award. Joseph Henry, director of the Smithsonian Institution, said it was "the greatest marvel hitherto achieved by the telegraph."

Left: Alec's exhibitor's pass was punched only once. He did not spend much time at the "greatest exhibition of science and technology ever assembled." He rushed home to grade his students' exam papers on time.

As much as Alec wanted the newly formed Bell Telephone Company to grow, he wasn't obsessed with getting rich. He wrote to Mabel, "I want to get enough [money] to take off the hardships of life and leave me free to follow the ideas that interest me most."

Alec and Mabel were married in the Hubbards' living room on July 11, 1877. For a honeymoon they sailed to England. A lighthearted Alec, deprived of music for so long by his telephone work, entertained the passengers for hours at the ship's piano.

Alec hoped to promote the telephone in England and got an assist from royalty. Queen Victoria asked for a personal demonstration.

Alec shocked everybody when he took the Queen's arm to get her attention. Touching the Queen was unacceptable, but Alec was forgiven because he was the inventor, the proud father of the most remarkable communications device ever seen.

Before the telephone's invention, telegrams were the fastest way to send a message. A person went to a telegraph office and handwrote a message that was translated into code. It was sent by wire to another office where it was copied by hand and, finally, delivered like a letter. It could be hours, even days, before the message arrived.

To sit in a living room and talk to another person miles away was an unusual, unexpected experience for everybody, including the Queen. She wanted phones installed immediately to connect her castles. And, of course, everybody wanted what royalty had.

Left: These wedding portraits of Alec and Mabel were taken during their honeymoon in England. There are no photographs from their actual wedding.
Right: Queen Victoria, seated in the center, described the telephone as "most extraordinary."

Thousands in England and Scotland paid to hear Alec demonstrate the telephone and lecture on Visible Speech. Important people invited the Bells to parties, but Alec needed more. He needed new challenges.

The father of a deaf child asked him to help organize a school in the Scottish coastal town of Greenock. Alec saw an opportunity to create a teaching program that would be a model for all deaf education in Britain.

In May 1878 Mabel gave birth to a daughter, Elsie May, and the Bells decided to stay in Europe until the baby was six months old. This gave Alec time to open the school.

It had only three students, and he taught them for less than a month, but teaching once again satisfied Alec immensely. "I have been so happy in my little school, happier than at any time since the telephone took my mind away from this work." He told Mabel that he'd always be known as a teacher of the deaf, but his life would never be that simple again.

Alexander Graham Bell returned to the United States to find that he would always be a public figure with public obligations.

Public demand for telephone service was intense. The maps below show that between 1890 and 1917 the Bell network wired almost the entire country. By 1885 this maze of telephone poles and wires added to the congestion of Broadway, in New York City (left).
Above: Samuel Clemens (Mark Twain) complained about his telephone service, but his 1881 bill shows that he had an extension phone.

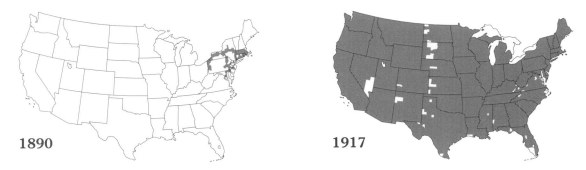

1890   1917

■ Counties connected to the Bell long-distance network

"The telephone reminds me of a child only it grows much more rapidly.... I see new possibilities before it— and new uses."

Above: Early telephone connections were noisy and filled with static. The Bell Company hired women operators to discourage customers from swearing.
Right: In 1892 Alec made the first call from New York to Chicago, opening a permanent long-distance network.

> *"The more fame a man gets*
> *for an invention, the more he becomes*
> *a target for the world to shoot at."*

A FRANTIC TOM WATSON met the Bells at dockside. Alec was needed in Washington to testify against the Western Union Telegraph Company. Western Union was selling telephones even though the Bell Company owned the patents.

The Western Union suit was just the beginning of the litigation. The right to claim invention of the telephone was tested in 600 different legal cases.

The principal witness for Bell Telephone had to be Alexander Graham Bell. Who but the inventor could prove he had invented the telephone? The printed records of those cases filled 149 volumes. Alec's testimony in just one case ran to almost 450 pages.

In the first suit, Western Union claimed that Elisha Gray, Alec's longtime rival, invented the telephone. Western Union dropped its claim and settled after Alec's lawyers submitted a letter, written by Gray himself, admitting that Alec was the sole inventor of the telephone. The Bell Company won this and every other suit, all 600.

In 1879 the Bells moved to Washington, D.C., to be closer to Mabel's parents. Their second child, Marian "Daisy," was born that year. Mabel was pregnant again in July 1881 when President James Garfield was shot. The Bells were summering in Massachusetts away from Washington's heat, but Alec was eager to help.

Alec often worked long hours in the study of his Washington, D.C. home. He could have been reviewing trial testimony, writing notes from an experiment, or answering the letter of a parent who wanted advice on educating a deaf child.

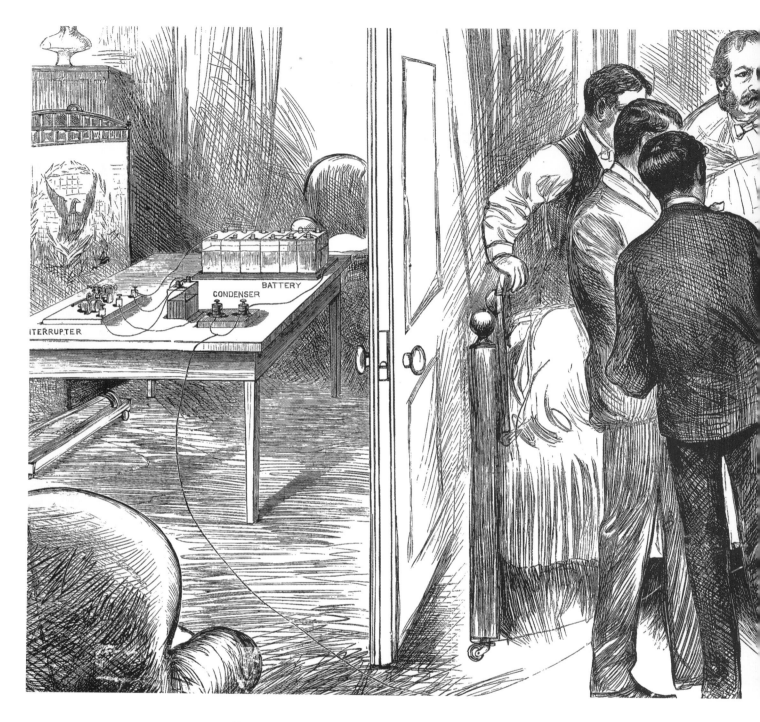

"Certainly no man can have a
higher incentive than the hope of relieving
suffering and saving life."

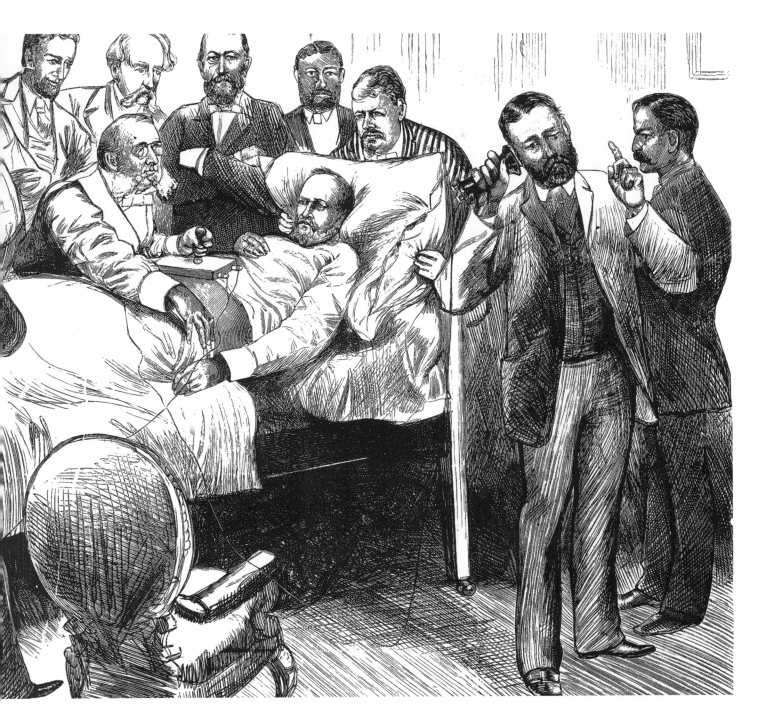

In this sketch a doctor passes a metal detector invented by
Alec across President Garfield's wound as Alec listens at right.
Several attempts to find the bullet failed, but another Bell
invention, the telephonic probe, would eventually help save the
lives of many soldiers. Not interested in making a profit from
human misery, Alec let another scientist manufacture the machine.

Before X-rays, there was no way find a bullet deep inside the President's body without making multiple incisions and hoping for luck. Could Alec invent an electrical device that would detect the bullet?

Alec worked furiously for weeks and developed two metal-detecting devices. Neither saved the President's life, but the second—a telephonic probe—was later manufactured and used in military hospitals for many years. It saved hundreds, possibly thousands, of lives.

A more personal tragedy led Alec to another life-saving invention. The Bells' son, Edward, was born prematurely. Unable to breathe by himself, the child died hours after his birth.

Mabel and Alec were stunned. They grieved greatly, and Alec resolved to see if he could prevent similar future tragedies. Less than a year later, he demonstrated his "vacuum jacket." Wrapped around the chest of somebody who couldn't breathe, it used a pump to force air into and out of the lungs—an artificial respiration machine. It was the prototype for the iron lung, which saved the lives of thousands of polio victims and is still used today.

These sketches from Alec's notebook show two artificial breathing devices: a vacuum jacket *(below)* and an air compression chamber *(left)*. He recorded every action and thought related to his work in notebooks which filled over 200 volumes. The first person to use X-rays in Canada, Alec made this one *(right)* around 1893.

"Make me work...at anything, it doesn't matter what...so that I may be accomplishing something."

FINANCIALLY, THE TELEPHONE made Alec and Mabel wealthy enough never to need to work again. But Alec was driven to invent, to work, to prove himself. He wrote, "I can't bear to hear that even my friends should think that I stumbled upon an invention and that there is no more good in me."

In 1880 France awarded Alec the Volta Prize for inventing the telephone. He used the $10,000 prize to underwrite the Volta Laboratory, which worked to improve Thomas Edison's phonograph. The phonograph recorded and played back sound on tin cylinders, but the sound was distorted and the cylinders wore out too quickly. The Volta Lab produced the floating stylus, or needle, and the record. The sale of patents on these inventions earned Alec $200,000 and allowed him to start the Volta Bureau, an association dedicated to

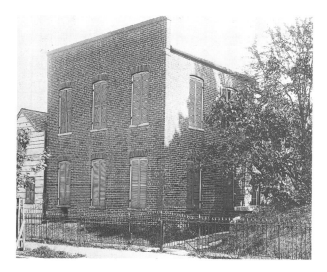

research and to publishing information about deafness. It eventually became part of what is now the Alexander Graham Bell Association for the Deaf.

Alec was never able to devote as much time to the education of the deaf as he wished. In 1883 he started a school for educating deaf and hearing children together, then had to close it because telephone court cases took so much of his time. But he always found time for deaf children, their parents, and their teachers.

Above: Alec's Volta Laboratory
Right: Helen Keller finger spells a message to Alec.
Blind and deaf, she became an international symbol of triumph over adversity. Keller's autobiography was dedicated to Alec, her lifelong mentor and friend.

The Bells needed a home away from the city. Alec craved privacy, solitude, and, most important, the cool weather of his youth in northern Scotland. Mabel wanted sun and sky and freedom from formality for herself and the girls.

They found it all in Baddeck, Nova Scotia, in 1885. Within a few years, they had purchased an entire peninsula and built Beinn Bhreagh (BEN VREE-ah), or "Beautiful Mountain" in Gaelic.

Beinn Bhreagh became a second home and gave Alec a platform for larger experiments.

"The study of Nature is undoubtedly one of the most interesting of all pursuits. God has strewn our paths with wonders, and we certainly should not go through Life with our eyes shut."

∽◯◯

Alec flies a giant tetrahedral kite in 1908 as his
grandson Melville *(center)* runs along underneath it.
Through his kite experiments he came up with
the tetrahedron—a pyramid-like group of triangles
that was lightweight but strong. He predicted its
use in "all sorts of constructing."

Alec had been intrigued by bird flight since childhood. Now he had the time and place to experiment with kite flying, which he thought would lead to safe aviation. He envisioned manned kites that would make soft takeoffs and landings.

Alec was very cautious. He experimented for almost 15 years before actually letting a person fly in one of his large kites. Those experiments, begun in 1891, were serious science, but Alec loved to combine work with play. Kites shaped like dogs and cows and elephants would glide across the starlit sky, entertaining the townsfolk who sewed the silk onto the frames.

After testing different shapes, Alec decided that the tetrahedron—four equilateral triangles joined together like a pyramid—produced the lightest and fastest kites. He realized that this same design could be used for building.

The tower he constructed at Beinn Bhreagh was incredibly light yet able to support enormous weight. Tetrahedral cells are common building blocks in space-frame architecture today. New York's George Washington Bridge was the first large structure to use Alec's innovation.

Alec recognized that his vision of slow but safe flight had no future when the Wright brothers flew their first biplane, an engine-powered, fixed-wing aircraft. Kites were safe, but biplanes would be faster as engine technology improved. Speed would win out.

Alec wanted to join in aircraft development, so Mabel, his best fan and supporter, started the Aerial

Right: Alec and an assistant prepare to fly a kite made up of pentahedral, or five-sided, cells.
Left: In 1907 Alec unveiled the world's first tetrahedral structure. This 70-foot tower was used as an observation platform during flight experiments.

Experiment Association (AEA) in 1907. Alec and four partners, all much younger than he was, successfully experimented with several aircraft designs.

The AEA made aviation history with these firsts:

Red Wing made the first public airplane flight in the United States.
White Wing was the first U.S. plane to use ailerons, or wing flaps, for stability and a three-wheeled undercarriage for smoother takeoffs and landings.
June Bug was the first plane to fly more than a half mile in public.
Silver Dart made the first heavier-than-air flight in Canada.

Glenn Curtiss, a partner in the Aerial Experiment Association,
sits behind the wheel of the *June Bug*, shown in flight above.
Curtiss went on to manufacture airplanes and
operate flying schools.

"I see no reason why
our mag[azine] should not be of
great popular interest."

Alec and his father-in-law, Gardiner Greene Hubbard, were dedicated promoters of science and learning. In 1888 Hubbard became one of the founding fathers of the National Geographic Society and its first president. After Hubbard's death in 1897, Alec, one of the Society's original members, was pressured into taking over the post.

The Society then was small. Its magazine was technical and of interest to very few. Alec's vision for it was much larger: The magazine

In 1888 these men *(above)* met in Washington to organize
a society "for the increase and diffusion of geographic
knowledge"—the National Geographic Society.
Right: Several years later aboard a ship off the coast of
Central America, Alec enjoys an issue of NATIONAL GEOGRAPHIC.

should publish "reliable and timely items relating to all the geographic topics that might be occupying the public mind." Its hallmarks should be "accuracy, general interest and 'dynamical' pictures."

When asked how he defined geographical subjects of interest, he projected his own interests onto the Society: "THE WORLD AND ALL THAT IS IN IT is our theme."

To achieve his goal, Alec recruited a talented young editor, Gilbert H. Grosvenor. With Alec's guidance and support, Grosvenor helped the Society become what it is today—the world's largest non-profit scientific and educational organization.

Grosvenor became part of the family when he and Elsie Bell married. Their son Melville Bell Grosvenor headed the National Geographic Society after his father's retirement. And Melville's son Gilbert is the Society's chairman today.

Above: Alec uses a toy to demonstrate the propeller
principle for his grandson Melville Grosvenor.
Left: Alec poses with his son-in-law Gilbert Grosvenor,
who was the editor of NATIONAL GEOGRAPHIC for 55 years.

*"Self-education is a life-long affair.
There cannot be mental atrophy in any
person who continues to...seek answers for
his unceasing hows and whys about things."*

A TEACHER SINCE HIS TEENS, Alec shared his love of learning with his grandchildren. He didn't instruct, he encouraged young people "to think, to experiment, to try things on their own." He developed a series of more than a hundred experiments in natural science that his grandchildren could do.

After dinner, he would often lead the family in popular song at the piano, letting his grandchildren turn the pages of music for him. Before turning in, he would read encyclopedia articles and take pleasure in how much there was to learn about the world.

Even in his 70s, Alec was hungry for achievement. After airplanes he turned to hydrofoils, boats that move above the water. At age 75 Alec received a patent for his hydrofoil improvements—64 years after

he invented a machine to separate wheat husks from the grain. Shortly before his death he went diving in a submarine tube to see underwater life in the Bahamas. His boundless energy and enthusiasm for invention, for science, and for finding the answers make his life an example worth following.

"There are no unsuccessful experiments," he said. "If we stop here, it is we who are unsuccessful, not the experiment."

Alec's HD-4 hydrofoil, which set a world water-speed record in 1919, speeds across Baddeck Bay *(above)*. At the dock Mabel asks Alec for a ride in the craft. Deafness never prevented Mabel from sharing a full life with her husband. An expert speech, or lip, reader, Mabel occasionally covered her eyes and told her grandchildren she couldn't "hear" when they made too many demands.

AFTERWORD

ALEXANDER GRAHAM BELL WAS NEVER CONTENT with the world the way it was. He never complained about it, he did something about it.

He is best remembered for the telephone, but his contributions to society and human knowledge—too numerous to list here in their entirety—go far beyond that invention.

He studied problems like the causes of deafness and invented the audiometer, a device that measures a person's hearing. His photophone carried sound over light waves, and he found a way to extract drinkable water from the air. He even warned of a "sort of greenhouse effect" that would result from burning fossil fuels.

Not every idea or invention was a success, but Alec had no fear of failure. He practiced a simple slogan that hung on his laboratory wall—"Keep on fighting." The advice that he gave to some students in 1917 was what he lived by:

Don't keep forever on the public road, going only where others have gone, and following one after the other like a flock of sheep. Leave the beaten track occasionally and dive into the woods. Every time you do so you will be certain to find something that you have never seen before. Of course it will be a little thing, but do not ignore it. Follow it up, explore all around it; one discovery will lead to another, and before you know it you will have something worth thinking about to occupy your mind. All really big discoveries are the results of thought.

This cartoon pictures Teddy Roosevelt "calling" home from San Juan Hill in Cuba over a thousand-mile-long wire. Today, cellular transmitters and receivers connect portable phone users.

60

CHRONOLOGY

March 3, 1847	Alexander Bell is born in Edinburgh, Scotland
1858	Adopts the middle name Graham; makes wheat-husking device
1862–63	Lives in London with his grandfather, Alexander Bell
1864	Builds speaking machine with brother Melville
1867	Brother Edward dies from tuberculosis
1870	Brother Melville dies from tuberculosis; family emigrates to Brantford, Ontario
1871	Begins teaching in Boston
1874	Experiments in Brantford with phonautograph; describes way to transmit sound through wire
1874–75	Works on harmonic telegraph in Boston with Tom Watson
June 2, 1875	Hears sounds through wire on harmonic telegraph
March 7, 1876	Granted U.S. Patent No. 174,465 for "Improvements in Telegraphy"
March 10, 1876	Famous first telephone conversation with Watson
June 25, 1876	First public demonstration of the telephone at the Centennial Exposition in Philadelphia
July 11, 1877	Marries Mabel Hubbard
1877–78	Honeymoons, lectures, and teaches in the United Kingdom; daughter Elsie May is born
1879	Moves to Washington, D.C.
1880	Awarded Volta Prize; daughter Marian (Daisy) is born
1881	Invents telephonic probe and vacuum jacket
1885	Visits Baddeck, Nova Scotia, future site of Beinn Bhreagh
1891–1908	Flight experiments at Beinn Bhreagh; Aerial Experiment Association established
1898	Becomes president of the National Geographic Society
1908–09	*Red Wing, White Wing, June Bug,* and *Silver Dart* airplanes make aviation history
1910	Begins hydrofoil experiments
1919	HD-4 hydrofoil sets world water-speed record at 70.86 mph
August 2, 1922	Alexander Graham Bell dies at Beinn Bhreagh of complications from diabetes; AT&T silences all telephones for one minute in tribute to Bell
January 3, 1923	Mabel Bell dies from cancer

BIBLIOGRAPHY

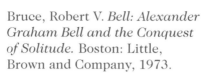

Bell, Alexander Graham. "Prehistoric Telephone Days." NATIONAL GEOGRAPHIC. (March 1922) 223–241. *

Boettinger, H. M. *The Telephone Book: Bell, Watson, Vail and American Life, 1876–1976.* Croton-on-Hudson, N.Y.: Riverwood Publishers, 1977.

Bruce, Robert V. *Bell: Alexander Graham Bell and the Conquest of Solitude.* Boston: Little, Brown and Company, 1973.

Bruce, Robert V. "Alexander Graham Bell." NATIONAL GEOGRAPHIC (Sept. 1988) 358–385.

Bryan, C.D.B. *The National Geographic Society: 100 Years of Adventure and Discovery.* New York: Harry N. Abrams, Inc., 1987.

Eber, Dorothy Harley. *Genius at Work: Images of Alexander Graham Bell.* New York: The Viking Press, 1982.

Grosvenor, Edwin S. and Weston, Morgan. *Alexander Graham Bell: The Life and Times of the Man Who Invented the Telephone.* New York: Harry N. Abrams, Inc., 1997.

Keller, Helen. *The Story of My Life.* New York: Doubleday, 1903.

Pasachoff, Naomi. *Alexander Graham Bell: Making Connections.* New York: Oxford University Press, 1996

Pelta, Kathy. *Alexander Graham Bell.* Englewood Cliffs, N. J.: Silver Burdett Press, Inc., 1989.

* This article, along with more articles by and about Bell, are available on a CD-ROM set called *The Complete National Geographic.* Ask your librarian about it and *Alexander Graham Bell: A Multimedia CD-ROM,* produced by Fitzgerald Studio, Sydney, Nova Scotia, Canada.

The "ghost" of Melly Bell visits his mother and two brothers in this very early experiment with double-exposure photography. Alec's love of photography led him to document his experiments, travels, and family life in pictures.

WORLD WIDE WEB SITES

These sites provide links to related sites:

Alexander Graham Bell Institute
http://bell.uccb.ns.ca/

Bell Labs Museum: History of the telephone
http://www.lucent.com/museum/1876ft.html

Alexander Graham Bell's Path to the Telephone, University of Virginia, Design and Invention
http://jefferson.village.virginia.edu/albell/homepage.html

ILLUSTRATION CREDITS

INDEX

Photographs are indicated by **bold-face.** If photographs are included within a page span, the entire span is boldface.

The world's largest nonprofit scientific and educational organization, the National Geographic Society was founded in 1888 "for the increase and diffusion of geographic knowledge." Fulfilling this mission, the Society educates and inspires millions every day through magazines, books, television programs, videos, maps and atlases, research grants, the National Geography Bee, teacher workshops, and innovative classroom materials. The Society is supported through membership dues and income from the sale of its educational products.
Call 1-800-NGS-LINE for more information.
Visit our Web site: www.nationalgeographic.com